SURVIVING AND THRIVING

DESPITE

THE
DRAMA

7 REMARKABLE STRATEGIES TO
REGAIN CONTROL, DEVELOP RESILIENCE,
AND REWRITE YOUR OWN HAPPILY EVER AFTER ENDING

MARSHA E. FRIEDMAN

Writing & Publishing Process by PlugAndPlayPublishing.com
Book Cover by Tracey Miller | TraceOfStyle.com
Edited by Jenny Butterfield

ISBN: 9781091667877

This book is dedicated to the strong women in my life who have been my friends, my mentors, and my supporters. I am grateful for their listening ears, their open hearts, and their guidance which helped me to survive and thrive despite the drama.

Table of Contents

Introduction 1

Chapter 1 Restoring Your Strength 7

Chapter 2 Releasing Your Emotions 17

Chapter 3 Rebuilding Your Connections 31

Chapter 4 Reclaiming Your Place 39

Chapter 5 Recapturing Your Optimism 49

Chapter 6 Rekindling Your Spirit 59

Chapter 7 Reframing Your Failures 69

Your Next Steps.. 79

Bonus Section: 10 Tips to Finding Love Again 81

About the Author... 87

Looking for a Speaker 89

Comeback Queen Playlist 93

Works Cited 95

Introduction

I have crowned myself the "Comeback Queen," not because I'm special but because I've comeback from everything life has thrown my way. I've pulled myself up time and again. I've overcome the challenges, roadblocks, and detours that life has thrown in my path. I've rebuilt my credit, rekindled my spiritual life, raised successful, independent children, reestablished my career, and reclaimed love again (and again). I'd rather my life was one of fairytale endings and happily ever afters, but I wouldn't be the person I am today without these experiences. There are moments when I wish for a boring, normal life without the drama, but I discovered that every crisis along the way had some lesson to teach.

Resilience is the Magic Ingredient

The biggest lesson of all has been resilience. I call myself the "Comeback Queen" because I have been blessed with an abundance of resilience, the capacity to regroup and realign, the grit and determination to not let anything stop me. Resilience is the ability to not only survive but also thrive when we are faced with change, especially uncontrolled, unexpected change. The life changes that impact us most deeply include serious illness, the loss of a job, financial distress, divorce, and death of a loved one. Resilience is our ability to not only fight our way back to a sense of safety, security, sanity, and control, but to also come back stronger than before.

How did I develop my resilience? Developing that quality wasn't easy; I did everything the hard way. I've been married twice, divorced and widowed, raised two children on my own, suffered debilitating migraines, and buried both my best friend and my second husband (both burials in a ten-month time span). Along the way, I declared bankruptcy, saw three of my siblings diagnosed with mental illness, lost both of my parents, accepted early retirement, and started a business. My life story wears me out, and I wish I could skip over all of these yucky parts.

This wasn't what my life was supposed to be. I grew up in the 1960's, "the good old days," when families gathered around the television to watch *Ozzie & Harriet*, *Leave it to Beaver*, and *Walt Disney*. The "American Dream" was a two-parent household with 2.5 children, a father who worked, and a mother who stayed home and raised the children. It looked so easy. Every problem had a solution. There was always a silver lining to all of life's challenges. That was the life I had. My father worked, my mother stayed home and raised the four of us kids.

I thought I would grow up, go to college, get a job, find my Prince Charming, and live happily ever after too. But real life doesn't promise fairy-tale endings. "We all deal with loss: jobs lost, loves lost, lives lost" (Sandberg & Grant 41). The question is not if these life challenges will happen but when. And when they do, the question for each of us is, "How will we face them?" Will we survive or thrive? Will we live under a storm cloud? Or will we work our way back to our own version of a fairy-tale life? The difference between living under a storm cloud and living a fairy-tale life is "faith, trust and a little pixie dust" (Barrie).

What Does It Take to Make Your Own Comeback?

Time and again as I have struggled through my life story, these seven strategies brought me through even the toughest situations. In each chapter that follows, I'll share what I've learned and how you can use these seven strategies on your journey to recovery.

1. Restoring Your Strength – How do you deal with the pressure of everything that's weighing you down? It's tempting to indulge to take the hurt away for a little while. Whatever you do to mask your pain may be making you weaker and could be compounding the challenges that you are facing. You need to be physically strong to work your way back to wholeness. In the chapter, you'll learn what fuels your physical energy as well as how to rebuild your strength and harness your inner power to restore your self-image.

2. Releasing Your Emotions – As you work through the obstacles on your path, you'll need to make room to face and embrace the roller coaster of emotions that will be coursing through your being. Stuffing your emotions inside and holding them at bay fuels a fire inside that will explode without warning. That explosion of emotion has unwanted repercussions and hits whomever wanders by at that moment. In this chapter, you'll learn about the connections between feelings,

thoughts, and behaviors, the phases of the grief cycle, and how to find comfort in opening yourself up to your feelings.

3. Rebuilding Your Connections – When we feel like victims in our own lives, taking on the role of the martyr and doing everything ourselves is tempting. But our friends and family want to help and support us when we need their support the most. They just don't know what to do, and we don't know how to tell them. In this chapter, you'll learn how to ask for and accept help to get the assistance you need.

4. Reclaiming Your Place – When you are in crisis, you feel like the center of the universe, the object of unwanted attention. We don't want to share our emotional distress with anyone else, and so we withdraw. We don't want to talk to anyone or engage in any activity that might be fun, or that fun will remind us of what's different in our lives. In this chapter, you'll learn how to shift your attention from the inside to the outside and gain a sense of fulfillment and self-worth.

5. Recapturing Your Optimism – How do you view the world, as an optimist or a pessimist? Your outlook colors how you view your own situation and will support your recovery or hold you back. Little problems become much larger when we look through a negative lens. In this chapter, you'll discover how to change your perspective and recognize the gifts in your path.

6. Rekindling Your Spirit – When we are facing disappointments and despair, it feels like no one is listening, not even God. It feels like our prayers, no matter how

heartfelt, can't be heard and won't be answered. In this chapter, you'll learn how to reopen those communication channels and rekindle the spiritual fire within.

7. Reframing Your Failures – When we fail or face a challenge, we often see ourselves as the cause. These personal failures are setbacks that make us say things like, "Woe is me, why me, or I'm a failure." In this chapter, you'll learn how to reframe failure, counteract your negative self-talk, and accelerate your recovery.

Your Journey Starts Here

As you begin your journey to wholeness, think about the persona you will take on when you break through to the other side. My "Comeback Queen" comes complete with a tiara, an anthem, and a playlist.

Who is the hero/heroine of your story? Will you be the Brave One, the Relentless Restorer, the Soaring Star, or the Sparkling Sun? Pick a persona that appeals to you, and let that "future you" support you on your journey to serenity and fulfillment. Or feel free to share the mantel of the Comeback Queen.

What's your anthem? Mine is "Brave" by Sarah Bareilles. In fact, I've created a complete 36-song, Comeback Queen playlist that I've been listening to as I write this book (included in this book on page 93). What's on your playlist?

Chapter 1
Restoring Your Strength

"In order to truly give to others,
you have to give to yourself first."

-Ali Vincent

Right now, you may be feeling down and defeated or stressed and overwhelmed, and seeing how or when life will get better may be a challenge. How do you deal with the pressure of everything that's weighing you down? Some people eat too much, some eat nothing, some drink too much, and some take medications. Some people smoke too much, and some people work too much. Taking the hurt away for a little while by indulging is tempting, numbing the sadness, pain, and loneliness with food, alcohol, and/or medications. Whatever you do to mask your pain and avoid your new reality may be making you weaker, and these indulgences could be compounding the challenges that you are facing.

I'm a food-aholic (dark chocolate and sweet-and-salty foods call my name) and an emotional eater, a deadly combination. I can easily fill my life with food to plug some imagined void. When I am feeling overwhelmed, depressed, sad, tired, and lonely, I will raid my kitchen looking for the "right" combination of food and drink to fill my empty spaces.

This pattern of binge eating was exacerbated after my husband passed away. I found myself eating in front of the television every night. I couldn't sit at the dining room table by myself; the experience was too empty, alone, and isolating for me. Instead, I set up a tray table in the family room and ate my meals in front of the television. My dinner companions were the newscasters and reporters who kept me up-to-date and the movie and TV show characters who entertained me. I became a binge watcher and quieted the pain with mindless eating.

To compound my poor eating habits, I started drinking with a neighbor. She was widowed a few months after me, and we took comfort together in sharing a glass or two of wine every night while reminiscing about our spouses. Polishing off an entire bottle of wine and then opening a second was nothing for the two of us. Before long, the wine became a necessity, even on nights when my neighbor didn't come over.

That's when I decided it was time to focus on myself. What I realized was that just like the safety announcement at the beginning of every airline flight, "If you are travelling with a child or someone who requires assistance, secure your mask first, and then assist the other person" – healing starts with me. The same is true in any situation. Before taking care of anyone else, you need to take care of yourself by rebuilding your strength and self-image. How did I rebuild my strength and self-image?

Call a Time-Out

First, I freed up my time, so I could focus on my mental and physical wellbeing. Several months after my husband's death, a colleague asked me to lead a program on women in leadership. While I was flattered by the offer and knew that the work was right up my alley, I also knew that the thought of taking on one more project was more than I could bear. Simply thinking about the additional work took my breath away. In fact, this realization brought me face to face with the reality that I needed space and time to heal. That night, I resigned from all of my outside, volunteer activities: leadership positions in three organizations and memberships in two clubs.

Whether you are training for a marathon or pushing through your weight training workout, you need mental focus to succeed. Running an extra half-mile or pushing yourself to finish that last rep takes both physical energy and mental stamina. Just like football or basketball coaches during a game when the pressure is on, you might need to call for a time-out. This time-out is your opportunity to step away from the commitments of everyday life and give yourself the space to begin the healing process. It takes time and focus to recover, reenergize, reassess, reconsider, and relax. No one is suggesting that stepping away should become permanent, just give yourself room to breathe and think.

Taking this time-out from programs, projects, and organizations gave me the space that I needed to concentrate on myself and my new situation. I gave myself permission to be selfish with my time and to redirect my energy and efforts towards healing. Only when I felt more settled in my new life did I reevaluate my priorities and recommit to some but not all of my previous obligations.

Fuel Your Body with Nutritious Foods

Second, I focused on what I was eating. Listen, we can *survive* by eating almost any type of food. But if we want to *thrive*, we must become conscious of what we are putting in our mouths, how often we eat, and the quality of the ingredients we use. As we age, this becomes even more critical.

No one can dictate how you should eat, that's your decision, but please give some serious thought to how you fuel your engine. Start slowly by paying attention to how you feel before and after every meal.

Before you eat a meal, rate your level of hunger on a scale of 1 to 5 (with 1 being "not hungry" and 5 being "ravenous") and ask yourself:

- Am I eating because I'm hungry or because it's time to eat?

- Is the food that I am about to eat fuel or comfort food?

After your meal, rate your level of satiation on a scale of 1 to 5 (with 1 being "slightly hungry" and 5 being "uncomfortably stuffed") and ask yourself:

- Do I need or want more food?

- Did this meal satisfy me? If not, what's missing?

- Did this meal give me the physical energy and mental focus I need right now?

- How happy or unhappy is my gut?

Listening to your body is important, and not only that, listening to your body is infinitely wise. Ask yourself the above questions, and listen carefully to your body.

Next, consider getting processed food and sugar out of your house and eating at home more often. Processed foods contain high levels of sugar often hidden in the list of ingredients like corn syrup, glucose, fructose, and maltodextrin to name a few. In addition, the chain restaurants are serving us foods engineered with salt and sugar to make them more palatable and enticing us to overeat. Based on the obesity rates in this country, the chain restaurants and processed food manufacturers are quite successful with their marketing and product development endeavors.

Last, try eating a diet that is high in proteins, fresh fruits and vegetables, and healthy fats. I find when I fuel my body with healthy unprocessed food, I feel and look better. My skin glows, my gut is happy, and I have more energy and greater focus to do what I need in my daily life. While you may not be able to make all these changes at one time, start small. What one, baby step can you take to improve your diet? Here are some ideas:

- Eliminate sugary desserts and eat fruit instead

- Try one new vegetable every week

- Eat at home five nights a week

- Learn how to order healthy meals when eating out

- Choose to eat local: locally grown food and locally owned restaurants

- Eat breakfast

- Add one, healthy snack a day

- Swap out diet soda and drink tap or sparkling water with lemon

- Forgive yourself when you fall off the wagon... and then get back on quickly

Move Your Body and Boost Your Energy

Finally, I focused on how I moved. To me, moving is as important to life as breathing. I am a devoted exerciser. When my children were small, I exercised before going to the office every morning, Monday through Friday, at the Jewish Community Center. I swam laps three days a week and lifted weights two days a week. Then I got divorced. Without the luxury of a spouse at home to wake up the children, get them dressed, make their lunches, and take them to school or the babysitter's house, how would I continue my workouts?

I invested in my own equipment – starting with a relatively inexpensive stationary bicycle. I worked out in the privacy of my bedroom every morning before waking up the children. As the years passed, I needed a wider variety of activity, and I found a used Stairmaster in the classified ads. Today, I have a full gym: Stairmaster, exercise bike, weight bench with free weights from eight pounds to twenty-five pounds, as well as an exercise ball and yoga mat. When the gym where I had been working out for the past few years closed, I simply rearranged my basement and "Marsha's Fitness Center" opened for business the next day. I didn't miss a beat or a workout.

I still workout six days a week, alternating between aerobics and weight training. Exercise centers me, gives me time to read, helps me feel energized, keeps the blood flowing, and enables me to keep up with my nine grandchildren. My goal is to keep the "Grandma arms" – loose skin dangling from the triceps – at bay, permanently!

In addition to working out at the gym, I look for opportunities to add extra fitness into my day.

- Taking a walk around the block when I go out to get the mail

- Parking my car a bit farther from the office or store

- Walking all of the aisles in the grocery store, even if I'm not doing a full shopping that day

- Engaging with family and friends in active play – swimming, walking, hiking, biking, hide-and-seek, etc.

- Comparing the step count on my Fitbit to my granddaughter's and working to keep up or, occasionally, beat her numbers

- Getting up and walking around the house or up and down the stairs at least once an hour when I'm working to give my eyes a break and to raise my heart rate

- Doing exercises at my desk while I'm writing

There is another benefit to increasing your exercise: exercise will keep you younger. Since losing my husband and reaching my 60's, I've been looking for a way to turn the clock back. I no longer gauge my age in years, instead, I track my fitness age. Fitness age analyzes how efficiently your body takes in and uses oxygen. I'm proud to say that I clock in at 39... to me, exercise is a virtual fountain of youth!

Want to find your fitness age? Go to WorldFitness-Level.org and answer a few simple questions. This fountain of youth does come with a warning. If your fitness age is above your chronological age, you have a high risk of dying prematurely. Your body is telling you to get up and get moving!

Review and Recommendations

You need to be physically strong to withstand the onslaught of emotions and the challenges you will face while working your way back to wholeness. Remember, the healing process starts with you. You can't help the ones you love until you are strong enough to stand on your own. Implementing the keys to fueling your physical energy and harnessing your inner power will supercharge your recovery.

Ask yourself these questions to determine where to start:

- How can I create the time and space I need to begin?

- How strong do I feel physically and mentally?

- What's fueling my body?

- How does my diet stack up? How much processed food do I eat?

- Who can guide my new eating plan?

- How do I keep myself energized?

- Who can partner with me on a fitness program?

- Can I find a work-out buddy?

- Who can I ask to support me or partner with me as I go down this path?

Once you answer these questions, answer one more: what one small step I can take today to begin my journey to recovery? And then set a date and time to get started.

"Good nutrition and regular exercise definitely help you cope with life's dramas."

-Terri Irwin

Chapter 2
Releasing Your Emotions

"Sometimes I feel like a human pin cushion. Every painful emotion hits me with ridiculously exaggerated force. And the anxiety feels like hands inside of me, squeezing my guts really hard."

-Juliana Hatfield

Regardless of which life-altering event you are facing, your emotional state for the foreseeable future will be anything but stable. Your feelings can quickly move from gladness and delight to irritation, frustration, and disappointment. Or you could be experiencing conflicting emotions at the same time. You might be glad that you are getting divorced but simultaneously be anxious about the impact of the divorce on yourself and your children. The road to resilience is paved with the ups and downs of the emotional roller coaster. Understanding the connections between our thoughts, feelings, and behaviors will help you smooth out the bumps and curves in front of you in healthy ways rather than self-medicating or stuffing down your feelings.

In Judaism, when a loved one dies, we light a candle that burns for a full, seven days during the first mourning period called Shiva (Hebrew for seven). At the end of Shiva, when the candle burns out and visitation ends, there is a sense of finality and heaviness. The end of Shiva begins the transition to a new reality. For me, that reality after losing my husband was widowhood, being all alone in an empty house, knowing that I would be a "plus one" to my couple friends, and that there would be no one to share the joys and challenges of daily life. Just thinking about this made my body start to shiver and made me want to lash out at the world.

This poem poured out of me that first day. Writing helped me capture the emotions I was feeling in images and memories. This poem was a baby step toward accepting the sadness, emptiness, and loneliness that I felt and a beginning to my journey of emotional exploration.

What's Left When the Flame Goes Out?

The questions

The misery

The despair

The heartache

The loneliness

The memories

The smiles

The hugs

The kisses

The embraces

The pain

The sorrow

The wondering why

The knowing

The guilt

The hurt

The family

The friends

The stories

The successes

The disappointments

The legacy

The traditions

The illusions

The struggles

The accolades

The sadness

The emptiness

The stunned silence

The quiet

The void

Nothing we can do will stop the onslaught of emotions coming at us during times of change and drama. No matter the source of the loss that you are facing, the emotional roller coaster that you are on won't stop running until you work through each of the ups and downs that occur along the way. I call this chapter "Releasing Your Emotions" because it provides the path to acceptance and healing, releasing you to move forward.

What are you feeling? Can you name each emotion? Are you sad, hurt, disappointed, frustrated, angry, depressed, hopeless, scared or [fill in the blank]? Are you wearing your emotions on your sleeve, or are you stuffing them back down into the darkness? Are you letting yourself smile and feel happiness, or are you quickly shoving those feelings aside to let the sadness, hurt, anger, and pain take over?

Pushing our emotions back down only backfires on us in the long run. We explode in anger, lashing out at the ones we love, or we take risks and make decisions that aren't in our best interest. Naming the emotions you are feeling is critical to your healing. This is not the time to be stoic but to let your emotions come out. "Recognizing emotion means developing awareness of how our thinking, feeling (including our physiology), and behavior are connected" (Brown 48). There is a cycle that connects our thoughts, feelings, and behaviors. Our thoughts determine our feelings, our feelings influence our behaviors, and our behaviors reinforce our feelings. This cycle of thoughts, emotions, and behaviors can be a positive or negative merry-go-round. In order to change our outcomes, we have to start by changing our thinking.

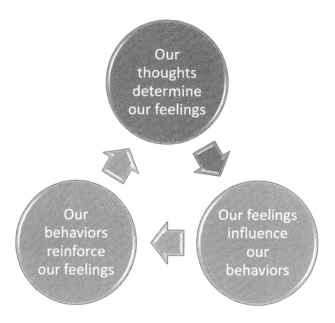

The Five Phases of Grief

Regardless of which life change we face, the bumpy road from denial to acceptance is the same. You will run through the full gamut of the grief cycle as defined by Elizabeth Kubler-Ross, MD, in her book, **On Death and Dying**. Here's a summary of the five-phase grief cycle:

1. Denial – Not accepting what has happened puts us in a state of shock and denial; we are stunned, over-whelmed, and numb. Nothing makes sense anymore. This phase enables us to get through our struggles one day at a time.

2. Anger – In this phase, we project anger at anyone and anything, even the universe. We lash out at the world, anyone who disagrees with our view, anything that up-

sets our day. Anger provides a framework to channel our frustration and despair in the face of loss. This emotion gives us strength of purpose and a path to survival.

3. Bargaining – This is the phase where we look at all of the "if onlys" and "what ifs" to wish for a different outcome to the situation. We attempt to bargain for an alternate reality rather than the one we are facing. We explore all of the things we could have done differently and wallow in the guilt of the "if onlys." There is never one "if only" or "what if," we must process the full range of options to accept the outcome.

4. Depression – During this phase, we can't or won't get up in the morning. We feel sad and lethargic, cry or want to cry. We feel hopeless and lost, have trouble sleeping or sleep too much. We don't want to eat or eat and/or drink too much. And we typically feel as though we "cannot stop the river of tears that overflows at strange, sometimes inappropriate, moments of the day" (Greyber). In other words, we are out of balance. Noting that this depression is not a form of mental illness but a fitting response to our enormous loss is important to our healing process.

5. Acceptance – During this final phase, we make peace with the loss and start moving on with life. We accept the new reality of life, the new normal. We adjust to new surroundings, new relationships, and new daily patterns. We are capable of accepting our feelings, responding to our own needs, and engaging with the world again.

There is no timeline or even order of how we go through the phases of grief. Some phases can happen simultaneously, or we can move back and forth through the stages. That movement can be quick or slow. The process is as individual as we are and varies based on the change with which we are struggling as well as the internal and external support we have along the way.

For example, three years after my husband's death, I felt stuck in the grieving process, unable to break through to acceptance. What was holding me back? The house that my husband and I had built together as our "forever home." I felt stuck in a loop of anger and depression because I was rattling around in a house that didn't feel like a home anymore. We planned to stay there for the rest of our lives, and his life ended too early. I wasn't prepared for him to move on, and somehow, my husband's presence in that house felt more palpable because of his absence. Leaving that house was a difficult decision. Astonishingly, I put the house on the market with no clear idea of where I would go; I simply trusted the universe to help me find my next home. After the move, I was able to finish grieving and find peace.

Working through the five phases of the grief cycle is an exercise in developing resilience. I think Sheryl Sandberg and Adam Grant in their book, **Option B**, said it best: "Resilience comes from deep within us and from support outside us. It comes from gratitude for what's good in our lives and from leaning into the suck. It comes from analyzing how we process grief and from simply accepting grief" (Sandberg & Grant 29). I would add that resilience also comes from having the fortitude to persevere even

Survivor's Guilt

If you are struggling with losing a loved one, one emotion that's not part of the grief cycle but can impede our journey to wholeness is guilt. As survivors, we often feel guilty. "Surviving feels like a sin, like I have stolen something I do not deserve" (Greyber). I had survivor's guilt. Thinking through our last days together filled me with both guilt and regret. I carried guilt for words not spoken and feelings not shared. I felt regret for actions not taken. My husband's sudden death took with it any opportunity to finish what we started or to say "goodbye." Our communication abruptly became one sided.

If he was alive, I would have asked for his forgiveness; instead, I had to ask myself for forgiveness. I knew that I had a choice. I could remain stuck, bargaining with the universe for an outcome that didn't exist. Or I could forgive myself and take the lessons from my regrets forward in my life. I chose to forgive myself by letting the regrets go and pledging to be more compassionate and more flexible.

This letting go and pledging to change my behavior enabled me to soften the guilt and move into acceptance. Moving on was challenging, but staying in place would have held me hostage to the guilt.

when the grieving process takes us to places that we'd rather not go.

Healthy Ways to Ride the Roller Coaster of Emotions

Again, whether you've lost someone close to you or you've experienced illness or financial struggles, your life will be littered with events that cause you to ride a roller coaster of emotions. However, it's not the events themselves that help you uncover your resilience – resilience comes from finding a healthy way to handle the emotional ups and downs.

So, how do you cope with the jumble of emotions that comes your way? First, I recommend you find a counselor or confidante who will let you vent your feelings and redirect those emotions into a positive action.

I started seeing a counselor eighteen months before my divorce. It took me a long time to face the reality of my situation. I tried to blame my unhappiness on my job, my volunteer work, being a working mother, anything other than the marriage. Reverting back to my fairy tale view of life, I was "never" going to be a single parent. I was going to be married for life, like my parents and their parents. When I worked through the pain, I had to face the reality and the guilt that my marriage was crumbling. An unbiased, third party like a counselor can walk you through the difficult journey of discovery.

Can't afford or don't have time for counseling? Try journaling.

Journaling has no rules. Use a notebook, loose-leaf paper, or buy a journal and any pen that feels good in your hand. Use colored pens or pencils if you choose. You make your own rules. Use whatever helps you express yourself: words, pictures, photographs, doodles, magazine clippings. You can journal anytime that works for you: mornings, evenings, weekdays, weekends, daily, weekly, monthly.

Journal when you have time, or journal when you have something you want to work out. "Turning feelings into words can help us process and overcome adversity" (Sandberg & Grant 62). I recommend writing long hand. There is something visceral and emotional in the act of writing. Don't worry – handwriting and spelling don't count, and no one else is going to read what you wrote.

In addition, feel free to collect poems, articles, quotes, drawings – anything that helps you to sort out your thoughts and feelings.

Journaling enables you to work through the full range of your emotions. If you are mad, feel free to vent or write a letter to the person who has wronged you. Just don't mail the letter. Instead, burn it. Writing a letter and burning the angry or regretful words has curative power. If you are sad, share your sorrow and let the tears flow. If you are frustrated or confused, write out the problem and brainstorm possible solutions. The key is to just write and let your thoughts go where they will.

What else can you do to work through your emotions?

- Listen to music to change your moods or set the tone for your day

- Beat your anger out in a pillow or yell and scream as loud as you can

- Dance to any music that suits your style when no one is watching

- Take a deep breath or count to ten when you feel like you are going to explode

- Watch a sad or a funny movie and cry or laugh to your heart's content – allowing yourself to feel your emotions (My movies of choice are **Beaches** and **Les Misérables**)

- Take a walk or a run in the park or around the block

- Go to the playground and swing on the swings

- Watch a sunrise or a sunset

- Start a meditation practice

- Find a place that brings you peace

- Take a vacation and give yourself the gift of time and space

- Visit the cemetery or wherever you feel closest to the person you lost

Embracing Emotions Over Time

Even after you have worked through the emotional turmoil of change and loss and reached acceptance and wholeness, there will be times when your emotions get out of control again. Most of the time, the memories of our loved ones and friends linger to comfort us. But at unexpected moments, something (a song, a story, a picture, a location, a book, etc.) triggers an intense emotional reaction. It's as if we are transported back in time to the top of our emotional roller coaster.

For example, I recently attended the funeral of a close friend's husband. In Jewish funerals, it is customary and considered a mitzvah (good deed) to shovel dirt onto the coffin because this act can never be reciprocated. Hearing the dirt hitting the lid and helping to cover the coffin was a haunting, visceral reminder which was like being hit in the gut. Suddenly, I was transported back to my husband's burial, and we were covering his coffin. I left the cemetery both sad and exhausted. This experience reminded me of those first moments of widowhood and the finality of my husband's passing.

How do you overcome these haunting memories? Don't go it alone. Phone a friend or loved one. I called my fiancé and asked him to spend the evening with me. I desperately needed a hug and someone to listen while I talked through my feelings and my memories.

The good news is not all of your emotional reactions will be haunting and hurtful. Some will be pleasant. Some will be funny. And some will be heart-warming.

Thanks to Facebook and the calendar, I think about my mother every year on September 17 - her birthday. Mom died in 2016 when she was 83. On the day that would have been her 86th birthday, I posted a picture of her on Facebook taken at her last birthday dinner. At the center of that picture is Mom, all smiles, with a large ice cream sundae in front of her. This picture epitomized her love of sweets. Mom was a tiny woman, not quite 5' tall, who in her last days of life survived on Graeter's coffee ice cream. We even served coffee ice cream at her funeral. Thinking about Mom on her birthday put a smile on my face and gave me comfort. Mom and I had a special bond, and although her last few years strained our relationship, I hold onto the memories of her, both the bitter and the sweet.

Recognizing that you won't always be in control of your emotional reactions is important. Let yourself experience all of the feelings that come your way, embrace them as they are part of your story. Once you have worked through the five phases of the grief cycle and built your resilience, be confident in your capacity to thrive and remain whole.

Review and Recommendations:

With the onslaught of emotions coming at us during times of change and drama, our challenge is to work through the ups and downs that occur along the way. Releasing emotions provides the path to acceptance and healing, releasing you to move forward. Ask yourself these questions to determine how you can get off the emotional roller coaster:

- Think about the life event you are facing and let your body take in your emotions. How would you label each one?

- Examine your emotions carefully. What part of your body feels each emotion?

- How does what you are thinking shape your emotions?

- How does your behavior connect to your feelings?

- Have you caught yourself lashing out in anger or frustration at your loved ones or pushing contentment and happiness away?

- Get a new perspective. In your mind, watch yourself from "the balcony," what do you see?

- Get the support you need. Do you have a counselor, therapist, or confidante to listen and guide you?

- How would you visually express your emotions? Try journaling, writing, drawing, doodling, and brainstorming to work through the emotions and to discover what's behind them.

- What can you do to challenge your negative emotions? Make a list of activities that bring you joy.

"Cherish your own emotions and never undervalue them."

-Robert Henri

Chapter 3
Rebuilding Your Connections

"You must do the thing you think you cannot do."

-Eleanor Roosevelt

Pride is a powerful emotion that can prevent us from moving forward in life. For example, when we're too proud and reluctant to ask for help, we get stuck in place and feel trapped. We think that we've been a burden on our friends, our family members, our co-workers, and others in our personal network.

After all, they've listened to us, they've fed us, and they've said, "call us anytime." But, when the time comes that we need help, we don't call. We don't want to impose our neediness on them (once again). We'd rather stay where we are than make an uncomfortable ask.

But this doesn't have to be the case. When we learn to ask for help, we can reap the rewards of our personal network. And do you know the best part about this process? Our personal connections want to help, and they will be grate-ful that you asked.

"What's the Worst They Can Say?"

Feeling lonely makes us act alone, and being alone at a time of need is not healthy. This feeling of isolation, with negative thoughts creeping into your brain, sets up a pat-tern of "woe is me" thinking that drags you down and makes you unable to move forward.

Our brains send us messages like "no one will help," "it's easier (quicker, cheaper, etc.) to do it myself," or "they won't do it my way." These thoughts make us feel like the victims in our own lives. When we feel this way, taking on the role of the martyr, retreating into our shells, and doing everything ourselves is tempting.

In the meantime, our friends and family who want to help stand idly by because they don't know what to do. The truth is that we don't know how to ask, and what's more, we aren't even willing to ask.

When I was a child and I hesitated to ask someone for help, my mother would say, "What's the worst they can say? No?" Having this mantra in my head, empowers me to ask. What I've learned is that if the ask is reasonable and possible, the other person will say "yes" much more frequently than "no." And, if necessary, the person you're asking will suggest an alternative to turn his or her "no" or "maybe" into a "yes."

Through the years, my friends often asked me, "How did you do it? How did you raise two children on your own?" I always answered that I didn't stop to think about the challenges that I faced; I put one foot in front of the other and kept moving forward. While that is true, as I look back now, two other truths stand out.

First, I know that if I had stopped moving, I would have become paralyzed with fear and unable to do anything. Second, I know that my family, my friends, and others in my network were willing to help me when I asked. My requests were rarely refused.

For instance, a year before my divorce, my ex-husband had dragged us through a bankruptcy, leaving me with no credit. Then, in the divorce, I got the house, the car, the kids, and the cats. Everything was good... except the fact that I needed to refinance a high-interest, mortgage loan (16%!) to keep the house. But I didn't let the bankruptcy keep me from searching for a way to refinance, get a lower rate, and keep my home. I contacted friends and neighbors to recommend a banker who was open-minded and had the latitude to work with my credit history.

Fortunately, I had a full-time job, and I connected with a banker who could see beyond the bankruptcy and view me as a good credit risk. It took time, but I slowly began to rebuild my credit. And more importantly, I was able to keep my children in the only home they had ever known.

Remember, the worst thing that can happen when you ask for help is someone telling you "no." I asked dozens of people in my network until I finally found a banker who was able to help me and my family. Did I let a few "no's" and "I don't know anyone" slow me down? No. I continued to ask for help until I found someone who said "yes."

Being willing to ask for and accept help from a variety of sources provides us with solutions and reinforces the connections we need not only to survive but to thrive.

Who Can You Ask for Help?

Take comfort in the fact that you don't have to do everything yourself. In fact, it's important to understand that asking for help is a sign of strength, not a source of weakness.

Knowing who you can turn to is critical to your recovery. Start by making a list of people you can call, including immediate and extended family members, friends, neighbors, co-workers, colleagues, teachers, clergy, congregants, acquaintances, club members, and anyone else you can think of in your personal network.

Don't forget to include professionals on your list. Over the years, I've used the services of lawyers, accountants, financial advisors, therapists, and insurance agents in my personal network. If you don't have a specific professional in your network, ask family and friends to help you connect to the right resource. Each of us has surprisingly large networks. Work your network and find the support you need.

Now that you have a list of names, add email addresses and phone contact information to make your list user-friendly. Don't feel that you have to create an exhaustive list. Keep your list small to begin and add the appropriate connections as needed. Just knowing that you have a list of names handy will empower action.

Once you have created your list, think about the skills, knowledge, and abilities of each person on the list. Knowing these specifics will help you decide who to call for a specific task. Figure out who can help you:

- Find a job

- Make minor home repairs

- Watch your children

- Get to work when your car is in the shop

- Work through a problem

- Celebrate life events

- Carpool

- Learn a new skill

- Pick up groceries or medications

- Fix your computer

- Take your pet to the vet

- Get to the airport

What other tasks do you need help with? Everyone on your list has his or her own strengths. Learning to leverage those strengths to help one another makes all of us stronger.

Now, match your list of tasks to the list of people who have the necessary knowledge and skills. Having a list handy will make your ask even easier.

How Do You Ask for Help?

So, how do you ask for help? The simple answer is to just ask. The more useful answer is to call, text, or email the individual with specifics about...

- What you need help with and the details of what you're looking for

- When you need help or when you need the task completed

- How you believe that they can assist you

Also, being flexible and open to their ideas and suggestions is important. Like I mentioned earlier, the person you're asking may suggest an alternative to turn his or her "no" or "maybe" into a "yes."

For example, when my husband died, over 300 people attended his funeral, and my home was filled to capacity with family and friends for the three nights of visitation that followed. All alone after everyone had left, I had a refrigerator full of food that I couldn't look at or smell because it conjured memories of the funeral. I just wanted the food to disappear, and I felt stuck. I didn't know what to do. So, I called my friend and she suggested calling non-profit agencies and gifting the food to someone else in need. She not only made the calls for me, she also brought her station wagon, filled her car with the leftovers, and drove me to a battered women's shelter. As soon as we made the donation, I felt like a weight had been lifted off my shoulders, and I could stand up straight again.

For some people, I know that asking for help can seem scary. But please realize that your "ask" is no different than asking for advice or information on LinkedIn, Facebook, or other social media platforms. Your friends and family will be delighted that you asked, and they will feel good that they were able to assist you in some small way.

Say "Thank You"

Be grateful. Say "thank you" for the help that you receive. Just smiling and saying thank you will go a long way in showing your appreciation. Alternatively, you could make a call, send a card, or give a gift card.

There are many ways to acknowledge the effort and show your gratitude. If you are stuck on what to say, here are some words of thankfulness that may spur your thinking. Thank you for:

- Helping me out

- Being there for me

- Including me

- Lightening my load

- Giving me a much-needed break

- Listening with an open heart

- Sharing your time with me

- Being so generous

Like I've mentioned throughout this chapter, your friends, family members, and personal contacts want to help you and will be grateful that you asked. All they really want in return is a simple "thank you." Show them that you appreciate them, and your gratitude will be remembered and treasured no matter how it is delivered.

Review & Recommendations

When you are willing to ask for and accept help, you can reap the rewards of connecting with your personal network on a deeper level.

To start the process, recognize that you need help. Consider where are you stuck and what's keeping you from moving forward. Remember, being willing to ask for and accept help is a sign of strength, not weakness.

Then, make a list of who you can ask and what skills, knowledge, and abilities they possess.

Finally, ask for help and show your gratitude with a smile and a sincere "thank you" when you find someone who is willing to help.

Every small, positive action enables you to move forward one, tiny step at a time. Following this simple process will ensure that you not only survive in tough times but thrive in all instances and that you will be one step closer to wholeness with the support and fortitude of others in your corner.

"Self-pity has one job and one job only:
it intends to stop us in our tracks."

-Julia Cameron

Chapter 4
Reclaiming Your Place

"We don't see the world the way it is,
we see the world the way we are."

-Anais Nin

When our lives are in turmoil, we act like turtles and pull into our shells. We don't want to share our emotional distress with anyone else, and so we withdraw. Our brains tell us that no one would understand our troubles or our pain and that we have to fix everything ourselves. We retreat from life and take comfort in licking our wounds alone. We don't want to talk to anyone or engage in any activity that might be fun or that will remind us of what's different in our lives. We hold ourselves separate from anything or anyone that might make us feel.

However, in protecting ourselves this way, we increase our stress level, and we rob the world of our presence and our value. That's why, in this chapter, we'll explore how to shift our attention from the inside to the outside and emerge with a new sense of fulfillment and self-worth.

Stress Kills

"A traumatic experience is a seismic event that shakes our belief in a just world, robbing us of the sense that life is controllable, predictable, and meaningful" (Sandberg & Grant 77). And in the process, unexpected and/or unplanned changes that come from a traumatic experience increase stress and anxiety, making us doubt our sense of security and safety.

Whether the life event is positive or negative, wanted or unwanted doesn't matter. Our stress levels react the same way regardless. We feel unstable and out of control. We don't know where to turn for comfort and reassurance, and as a result, we draw back into our shells and increase our alone time. And if that wasn't bad enough, according to Kelly McGonigal in her 2013 TED Talk, "How to Make Stress Your Friend" (McGonigal), this rise in anxiety and stress correlates to a 30% increased chance of dying. Why? Because most people handle stress in an unhealthy way. For example, are you handling your stress right now by:

- Eating too much?

- Sleeping too much?

- Hiding from life?

- Screaming, yelling, or having a temper tantrum?

- Ignoring what's going on around you?

- Drinking too much?

- Becoming a workaholic?

If so, then you're not alone. Most people inadvertently fall back on unhealthy habits when it comes to managing stress. But there are healthy ways for you to handle your stress and reemerge into the world. Let's look at six healthy alternatives for you to gain a sense of fulfillment and self-worth.

You Are Not the Only One

First, you must realize that you are not the first person to experience what you're going through. Others have had and are having the same experience you're having right now. I suggest finding these people and learning from them. How? You can connect with people who share your experience by finding a support group that focuses on the challenges you face.

There are support groups for people who are facing a variety of life changes from chronic medical conditions, divorce, and addiction to bereavement or job loss. Support groups provide research, learning resources, strategies, tips, and access to a group of like-minded and experienced people. In addition, support groups provide a safe place to disclose your feelings and concerns. Not only will you find others who share your challenges but also mentors who have walked the path you're on and are willing to impart their wisdom and their lessons learned. You'll gain hope and confidence by hearing from people who have been in your shoes and who are whole again.

I attended a Breast Cancer support group with my friend, Cheryl, early in her treatment. What I found was a group of women who felt comfortable revealing their pain, their treatments, their diagnoses, and their recoveries. The group was a place to get questions answered and to leave with hugs of caring and support. I walked away in awe of the power, grace, and electricity that permeated that room. The biggest lesson I took from that night was "don't go there until you get there," a phrase often repeated by those in treatment to keep focus on today and not on the "what ifs" of the future.

Take a moment and search for local support groups. When you find one that feels right, schedule a time to visit the group. You'll realize that you're not alone and there are people who can help shortcut your recovery.

Sharing Your Gifts with the People Who Depend on You

Think about the gifts you bring to the world. What are your talents and skills? Are you known for your planning or organizing ability, speaking or writing, cooking or baking, sewing or crocheting, technical wizardry or fix-it capabilities? What makes you stand out, and what do friends or family ask you to do? Once you identify those special talents and skills, think about how you can use them to help others and where you can find volunteer opportunities.

Each of us have talents and gifts we must share with those who depend on us - family, friends, neighbors, co-workers, pets, customers, suppliers, and our community. Sharing your gifts with your network will help you focus outside of yourself and provide a sense of fulfillment and self-worth. In addition, when you help others, your body releases oxytocin, a natural anti-inflammatory that heals the heart muscle and helps motivate you to find the help and encouragement you need.

Listen, each of us is a resource for our friends, our family, our neighbors, and our community. You don't have to take on a huge project, simply putting in a few hours of your time will give you a new sense of purpose and fulfillment. I'm part of a group of women who knit and crochet for charity. We make scarves, hats, blankets, and shawls for people in our community who are homeless or ill. This project helps me focus my thoughts outside myself, gives me a reason to leave home, and enables me to share my talents with the world.

What are your talents, skills, and gifts? How can you share them with your family, friends, neighbors and community?

Get Out of the House

Staying in your shell and inside your house is one of the worst things you can do, as staying alone feeds your loneliness and increases your chances of sliding into depression. Getting out of the house and being around others brings you out of your shell, so finding opportunities to go to lunch, grab a coffee, attend a lecture, see a movie, walk around the art museum, etc. with a friend or group of friends is important.

My late husband and I had season tickets at the theater, which I renewed after his death. I didn't know who would go with me, but I knew that just having those tickets would give me a reason to connect with friends who shared my passion for theater. At the same time, going to the theater would keep me connected to my husband's memory and help me find joy again.

What do you love doing outside of the house? Who can you call who shares your passions? Make a list of places to go and people who would love to go with you.

Can't think of anyone to go out with? Download the "Meetup" app and find a group of people who share similar interests. The benefit of "meet-up" groups is that the activities are designed for a group, and you won't be doing them on your own. Getting out of the house allows you to get out of your head and shifts your focus from yourself to a relaxing and healing pursuit, while giving you reasons to venture out into the world.

Reinvent Yourself

Transitioning from being part of a couple to being single is stressful. I've faced that transition twice, first through divorce and then as a widow. Admittedly, figuring out how to be single in a world that is designed for pairs was a challenge. When you become a single parent or a widow/widower, not only are you now alone, but most of your couple friends don't include you in their social plans. The women may be available to meet for lunch or to go shopping and the men for a round of golf or a beer. But their social lives are structured around pairs and you are the "odd" man or woman out. When and if you are included, you are a "fifth wheel," a sometimes awkward single in a world of pairs.

If you are now single and had been part of a couple, accepting your new reality and reinventing yourself in order to embrace your new identity is critical. I know, easier said than done. Fortunately for me, I had a friend who never married and who demonstrated to me how to be successfully single. To this day, she embraces her aloneness without being lonely and is a role model for anyone who's been single. She has a full life – family, friends, and personal interests – and she has taught me the there is no shame in being single. In fact, being single can be empowering. No one to report to, no one to check in with, no one to take up your time or change your schedule. You can use your time as you like. Accept invitations that come your way. Look for opportunities to pursue your interests and passions. And do what makes you happy and fills you with joy.

Over the years, I've been able to develop relationships with other women who were in my "club" – divorced, single mothers or single, never-married women. When my children were in grade school, another divorced mom and I became close friends, and our social lives became family dinners together and even joint vacations. We shared our hopes and dreams for our children as well as the frustrations of being a single parent and of dating. Since our children were in school together, we attended school plays, fundraisers, and other events as a team. We shared in the pride of our children's accomplishments as well as the disappointments when life didn't turn out the way we wanted.

It's never too late to reinvent yourself. In fact, I found myself in a constant state of reinvention to make myself a better person. Through my reinvention after divorce, I've even had women who are thinking about divorce call on me as a guide, mentor, and advisor. To this day, I'm available to anyone who is going through separation or divorce, trying to see what life after divorce will look like, and how to gracefully navigate the single life (with or without children).

Are You Ready to Find Love Again?

If you're single and want additional information on finding love again, I've included a Bonus Section on page 81 with my 10 Tips to Finding Love Again - my gift to you. Enjoy!

Change the Conversation in Your Head

One of the easiest ways to manage stress and shift your focus is to change the conversation in your in your head. How do you that? By asking yourself better questions. For example, rather than asking yourself, "why does this always happen to me" and playing the victim, ask yourself, "How can I use this experience to learn more about myself?" This simple change will empower you to find positive answers that help you reconnect and celebrate your true self. Asking better questions will also help you recognize and rejoice in your resilience.

Open Yourself to New Possibilities

After eight years of managing life as a single parent, I decided to take a course at the public library called, "The Artist's Way" – a twelve-week program on opening up to your own creativity. That class became a journey that helped me embrace my identity, forgive my mistakes, and reawaken my dreams. At the end of the twelve weeks, I rediscovered what made me feel pleasure, eliminated people and things that made me unhappy, felt more centered and empowered than I had in years.

Coincidently, during this class, I met and began dating my second husband. I believe that connection happened because I learned to open myself up to new possibilities.

What have you always wanted to do but have never done? What new possibilities can you open yourself up to? You can take up a new hobby, learn a new skill, or pick up an activity that you haven't pursued in years. For example, join a photography club, attend classes at the art museum, or connect with a biking or hiking club. Consider taking classes at a local community college – many offer a range of non-credit classes covering topics from yoga, religion, and meditation to film, history, and philosophy. Take some time now and brainstorm topics and capture ideas that appeal to you.

Review & Recommendations

In order to recover more effectively and reclaim our place in the world, we need to focus on healthy ways to reduce stress. In this chapter, you learned six healthy options to help.

- Recognize that you are not alone and connect with those who have walked the path you are on, and ask for their guidance and support.

- Realize that you have talents and gifts to share and find ways to use those gifts in service to others.

- Get out of the house and out of your shell by getting active and finding opportunities to share meals and experiences.

- Reinvent yourself by following your passions and doing what fills you with joy.

- Change the conversation in your head, ask positive questions that help you reconnect, and celebrate your true self.

- Open yourself to new possibilities, and watch your reality transform in front of your eyes.

Now it's time to implement these healthy options into your life. Each strategy is an opportunity for you to feel more stable and put yourself back in control.

"Whatever you think you can do or believe you can do, begin it. Action has magic, grace, and power in it."

-Johann Wolfgang Von Goethe

Chapter 5
Recapturing Your Optimism

"A pessimist sees the difficulty in every opportunity; an optimist sees the opportunity in every difficulty."

-Winston Churchill

Let's take a page from Winne the Pooh and visit the Hundred Acre Wood. Among the woodland creatures who are Christopher Robin's friends and companions are a donkey named Eeyore and a tiger named Tigger.

Eeyore is a sad, sullen fellow who constantly complains that it's been a rough week and nothing is going his way. Tigger, on the other hand, is joyful, outgoing, and self-confident, always bouncing around declaring what a wonderful fellow he is. The Eeyores of the world see their glass as half-empty and are considered pessimists. The Tiggers of the world see their glass as half-full and are considered optimists.

If your glass is half-empty like Eeyore's, then you tend to see the dark, difficult side of life and feel like you can't survive. However, if your glass is half-full like Tigger's, you have gratitude for the small things that make a difference in your life and an "I can do it" attitude.

So, how do you describe yourself? Are you more like Eeyore or Tigger?

By adopting a Tigger mentality, you can fill your well with joy and happiness to buoy yourself up against the high tides and hard times. You can face life's challenges, certain that you will come out whole on the other side.

Shifting your perspective is what we want to focus on in this chapter. We're going to explore five ways that can help you channel your inner Tigger and reclaim your optimism. Moving towards optimism can help you see and experience the pleasure and delight life has to offer every day and get you out of any funk you find yourself rolling around in.

Change Your Perspective

"Paying attention to moments of joy takes effort because we are wired to focus on the negatives more than the positives" (Sandberg & Grant 101). However, if your glass is half-empty and you are having difficulty seeing a path forward, changing your point of view can bring you unexpected positive changes.

When just getting up in the morning and putting one foot in front of the other seems impossible, give yourself the gift of a new perspective. Try viewing your life circumstances through a new lens. For example, you can pretend you are someone else (perhaps you know someone who personifies Tigger), and take a fresh look at yourself and your circumstances through their eyes. How would they react in your situation? What would they do differently? How do they continue to smile even when it's storming around them? What would they do to lighten their emotional, financial, or physical load?

Another option is to do some time traveling, picture a time months or years into the future, and envision how your life has changed for the better. What brought you to this place? Who is there with you? How is this picture different from where you are today? Look carefully, your next steps may be inspired by the differences.

Or go up to the "balcony" and see how the world looks from up there. Try to get the view from above. You decide the height of the balcony. You adjust the viewfinder to get the clearest image. What do you see from this height? How does that image affect your understanding?

Give one or all of these exercises a try, and see how a simple change in perspective affects your attitude and outlook on life. Which view brings the most clarity? What answers did you find there? What questions linger?

Create a Bucket List of Joy

"Seeking joy after facing adversity is taking back what was stolen from you" (Sandberg & Grant 99).

On the second anniversary of my husband's birthday after his death, I invited a few close friends over to watch the 25th Anniversary edition of **Les Miserables**. **Les Mis** was our favorite musical. We saw the show in Cleveland, New York City, and London and watched both the 10-year and

25-year anniversary shows multiple times. I couldn't think of a better way to honor his memory: watching **Les Mis** and eating hot fudge sundaes with whipped cream and nuts, an evening I knew that my husband would have enjoyed with great delight. Having this party in his honor helped me create joy on a day that could have been completely wrapped in sorrow.

Do you know what delights you? In the movie **Wild**, Laura Dern plays Cheryl Strayed's mother, and despite being a single mother raising two children, Dern's character takes pleasure from the simple things in life, like watching sunrises and sunsets and listening to music like Simon & Garfunkel's "Homeward Bound" and "El Condor Pasa." When do you feel moments of delight during your day?

Think about what fills your bucket with happiness and wonder. Make a list of the activities that help you feel renewed and refreshed. Here's my list to help you get started on your own "bucket of joy" list:

1. Read a book
2. Take a walk
3. Go to the art museum
4. Browse a bookstore
5. Go to the library
6. Get or give a hug
7. Pet the dog/cat
8. Work in the garden
9. Sit in the sun
10. Look at the moon
11. Watch the stars and planets
12. Drink a glass of wine
13. Go see a movie
14. Watch a play
15. Play with children
16. Play cards or a board game

17. Go to the zoo

18. Eat a hot fudge sundae

19. Make cookies

20. Bake a cake

21. Watch a sunrise or sunset

22. Listen to a thunderstorm

23. Throw a snowball

24. Make a snowman

25. Go skating or sledding

26. Go biking or hiking

27. Paint

28. Write

29. Exercise

30. Rearrange the closet

31. Invite friends to dinner

32. Listen to music

33. Light candles

34. Soak in a hot bath

35. Stay in PJs and binge watch a TV show

36. Visit a friend or neighbor

37. Sit in the backyard, eyes closed, and enjoy the sounds of nature

38. Go to a park or playground and swing on the swings, go down the slide, be a kid!

39. Repaint the bedroom

40. Take a drive through the park

41. Meditate

42. Take a yoga class

43. Watch a favorite movie

44. Toast marshmallows and drink hot chocolate

45. Crochet

46. Rearrange the furniture

47. Try a new recipe

48. Go to a new restaurant

49. Call an old friend

50. Go shopping

Many of these activities are small and don't take a lot of time, money, or effort but each one can add an element of delight into a dismal, challenging, or an otherwise ordinary day. Your list may be longer or shorter. I recommend keeping a copy handy in order to add to your list or to choose ways to fill those sad, stressful, or empty moments with pleasurable activity.

Combat "Less Than" Thinking

When we are trying to figure out what to do next or how to get out of the bed in the morning, our self-confidence shrinks and we feel "less than." Feeling "less than" sends us messages that we can't do anything right and that our lives will never be normal again. What's the best way to combat this "less than" thinking?

Chase away "less than" thinking by reinforcing your strength and self-worth. Make a list of your accomplishments, no matter how small. Start from your earliest memories. My list includes getting an "A" in an accelerated, summer-school math class in first grade and being the math wizard in my fifth-grade class, as well as serving as President of my children's school and being named Toastmaster of the Year in Northeast Ohio. When you are feeling low, look at your list of accomplishments, and let yourself feel the pride and pleasure of your achievements. Reviewing this list will enable you to say to yourself "You got this, you can do it!" and "You go, girl!" with confidence. Just like the Little Engine that Could, you can change the message in your head from "I think I can" to "I know I can."

Be Grateful

Another way to reclaim your optimism and be more like Tigger is to focus on being grateful. Focusing on gratitude stimulates positive thoughts and helps us bust through patterns of negative thinking.

I recommend creating a gratitude journal and starting each day by recording what you are grateful for. For example, I begin each day being grateful for my cat purring softly by my side. Yes, even the smallest things count. In fact, the small things are sometimes the most important. For you, that first cup of coffee or a hug from your spouse or child might be the most important.

You can also use your gratitude journal throughout your day and find moments to be grateful for. For example, pay attention to the times during the day when you say "thank you," hold a door open, or offer help to someone else. "True happiness is not found at parties or on a quiet beach. Through lenses filtered by pain, we learn to treasure great moments. We learn gratitude for the ordinary" (Greyber). Just tuning into the small ways that we show gratitude toward others will increase our own happiness.

Finally, you can use your gratitude journal at the end of the day to reinforce what's going right. Here are a set of questions to consider:

1. What went well today?

2. What lessons can I learn?

3. What small step did I take today to move forward?

When you are in the midst of a setback or major life challenge and every day seems to be filled with never ending disappointment and misery, read your gratitude journal.

Avoid BMWs & Hire a Negativity Cop

Even if you are not an Eeyore, you probably know and love some people who are. Avoiding those people with negative attitudes who bring you down is important.

Like Eeyore, they see and talk about what's wrong in the world and how nothing is going right. They look at the world through dark glasses. Spend an afternoon or evening with them, and you come home feeling worn down and exhausted. The problems you have become larger and more complex just being in their presence. I know that's what happens to me.

Think about the people in your life who fit this description. My nickname for these people is BMWs (bitchers, moaners, and whiners). I suggest making a choice to not spend time with them, or if avoiding them is unavoidable, then limit your exposure to their negative attitudes. You can walk away or tune them out. It's your choice. When you are working through your own challenges, you don't need their negativity piled on.

Another option is to consider hiring a "negativity cop" to keep you in a positive mindset. This negativity cop is a friend or family member who will hold you accountable for presenting a positive outlook to the world. This person will kindly and gently nudge you when you have fallen into the negativity trap and will help you climb back out. He or she has your best interests at heart.

Avoiding BMWs and finding people who lift you up, are willing to listen, and have a positive outlook on life, will help you change your attitude about life's ups and downs.

Review and Recommendations

As you leave the Hundred Acre Woods, channel your inner Tigger and your "you got this" attitude. Focus on the new perspectives you've seen of your situation and work on making them a reality. What did you see, hear, and feel in each of the perspectives you tried? What can you do to turn what you experienced into a reality?

Use your "bucket list of joy" to find delight on a daily basis. Give yourself the gift of pleasure whenever you have a few moments to yourself. When you have a "bucket list of joy" at the ready, finding delight is easy. Remember, happiness and contentment can be found in the smallest moments and those feelings can last for hours and days. How long is your "bucket list of joy"? What else can you add on?

Eradicate "less than" thinking by reviewing your personal accomplishments from the smallest to the most significant. Know that you are "all that" and so much more. Building up your self-confidence helps you feel secure in the knowledge that you have what it takes to recover and renew your life.

Show your gratitude for being alive each day. Begin your day by recognizing the good things that surround us, from the smallest gift, like a cup of hot tea, to knowing that our close friends have our backs. End the day with gratitude by recording what went well, the lessons learned, and giving yourself credit for taking steps forward.

Avoid or minimize the Eeyores in your midst who tend to be BMWs (bitchers, moaners, and whiners). Choose to walk away from them or tune them out if avoidance isn't an option. To ensure that you keep your own attitude up, hire a negativity cop to be your personal attitude assistant. These measures will help you maintain a positive, hopeful outlook.

"Our imagination is skilled at inhabiting the negative.
We must train it to inhabit the positive."

-Julia Cameron

Chapter 6
Rekindling Your Spirit

"Out of suffering have emerged the strongest souls; the most massive characters are seared with scars."

-Khalil Gibran

Life isn't fair... as a mother, I used this line with my children on a regular basis when they were complaining that one got more or was treated better than the other. I would often say, who told you that life was going to be fair? In 2009, my best friend, Cheryl was diagnosed with breast cancer. She wasn't the first of my close friends to get this diagnosis, but Cheryl's cancer was stage three and the kind that has a 75% recurrence rate. Definitely, not fair.

Where do you find hope in the face of that diagnosis and those odds? Hope comes from within us. Hope comes from the support and love of those around us. Hope comes from being grateful for each day. Hope comes from the simple blessings of waking up in the morning, having a cup of coffee, and getting a hug from our loved ones. Hope comes from the grit and determination we muster in order to deny the dire consequences of our diagnosis.

Rather than sit by idly and do nothing, I suggested signing up for the Susan G. Komen Breast Cancer Three-Day. The Three-Day is an event where you walk 60 miles in three days – a nearly impossible feat. For the privilege of walking, each participant must pay $90 and raise a minimum of $2300. Between Cheryl and I, we convinced four other women to sign up. Our team was aptly named the BFFs (Breast Friends Forever). With the amount of time required for training, seeing each other sweat, and sharing tents together, we developed the commitment that BFFs have to one another.

With the help, support, and love of our husbands, families, and friends, our team raised over $27,000 and was named one of the top-ten fundraising teams in the 2009 Cleveland walk. The Three-Day gave all of us something to focus on and to look forward to as Cheryl began her treatments – six months of chemotherapy followed by three months of radiation. Cheryl was one of the most positive people I've ever known, and her attitude kept us all smiling.

Cheryl remained hopeful in the face of her cancer diagnosis, chemotherapy, radiation, and surgeries. Her hope refused to wane, even when her cancer recurred in the winter of 2012. Cheryl survived to see her daughter get married and to welcome her first grandchild into the world. Cheryl denied her own mortality until the last day of her life, when she fell into a coma and passed on.

Faith Tested

Losing my husband just ten months after losing my best friend was devastating. I found it hard to eat, impossible to sleep, and breathing was a chore. I felt cheated, robbed, alone, and miserably lonely. I felt like a broken china doll with pieces missing. I desperately wanted to find my center, but I didn't know where to look or how to start.

Our faith is tested when life doesn't turn out the way we want or expect. We look to God to be strengthened and comforted through prayer. I went to synagogue and tried to pray but the tears blocked my prayers. I felt my husband's presence when I looked up at the windows near the holy Ark, but still I felt blocked. I desperately needed to mend the holes in my soul and heart, but there was something blocking my connection to God.

I wanted answers to all of my questions: Why did this happen to me? What did I do to deserve this fate? But I couldn't find the words, the prayers, the thoughts, the link to God. I was floundering in my anger, my grief, and my despair.

I turned to the book, **A Time to Mourn, A Time to Comfort** by Ron Wolfson, which covers death and mourning rituals in tremendous detail, but this book was silent on rebuilding one's faith. I had read **When Bad Things Happen to Good People** by Harold Kushner to help understand and accept Cheryl's death. I brought that book out again and reread the pages I had dog-eared, looking for guidance and answers to my new dilemma. I needed to know how to get past the emotional trauma that comes with sudden death.

I did not know where to turn. I met with my Rabbi, but he was more interested in telling me about the remodeling project that he and his wife were considering than in listening to my woes. This only added to my loneliness and my sorrow.

The Power of Hope

What is hope? Hope is the belief that things will get better. Hope goes beyond wishing to believing that positive change will happen. Obstacles in our path don't matter. Hope will remove them. Cheryl exemplified hope in every breath she took, in the way she approached every task, every challenge, every roadblock, every change. She made life look easy despite the pain, despite the treatments and their side effects, despite the disfiguring surgery and the uncomfortable recovery. She took everything in stride, and for those of us surrounding her, we got on her bandwagon. Cheryl believed she would survive, so we did too.

No matter your religious or spiritual beliefs, each of us benefits from hope. Here's a story from Rabbi Harold Kushner's book ***Conquering Fear: Living Boldly in an Uncertain World*** (Kushner 93). This story shows how in the face of the most difficult circumstances, hope sustains us:

> An unforgettable story from the Holocaust tells of a group of Jewish inmates in a Nazi concentration camp. It was the first night of Chanukah, the winter holiday recalls the victory of the weak over the powerful and of the few over the many in the 2nd century BCE. Chanukah always falls at the darkest time of year, and Jews mark it by lighting candles against the cold and dark. Holiday celebrations were forbidden in the camp, but one man saved a bit of the bread from his even-

ing meal, dipped it in grease from his dinner bowl, fashioned it into an impromptu candle, said the appropriate prayer, and lit the bread. His son said to him, Father that was food you burned. We have so little of it. Wouldn't we have been better off eating it? The father replied, my son, people can live for a week without food, but they cannot live for one day without hope.

How to Restore Faith

What is faith and how do you restore it? Faith is having an unwavering belief in something larger than ourselves. Faith comes to us from connection to our higher power, call it what you will, God, Allah, Buddha, or Jesus. Faith can also be found in the form of a loved one or a cause. Faith gives you a reason for existing. Faith starts with believing that you can overcome, you can be whole again. Faith helps you find center again.

Here are seven ways I've found useful to help rekindle one's spiritual life:

1. Connection points – When someone dies, we feel lost and we crave those lost connections. Where or when can you renew or recreate those emotional connections with your lost loved ones? This step may take some exploration. Where did you meet, talk, laugh, or interact most often? What did you share in common? Where are you when this person's name and face most vividly come into your memory? For me, I felt most connected to my husband when I was at the synagogue. I can't go into an ice cream parlor without thinking about my

mother and her love for coffee ice cream. And I think about my father when I am greeting someone, and I ask, "How are you doing today?" My father's constant silly retort, "compared to what," fills the space in my thoughts.

2. Show gratitude – Count your blessings every day for what you have in life and what you want, not what you've lost. Think about the people who fill your life with love and those who you love in return. Find time to express your feelings and to connect with others. Think about how you can honor the people who you've lost by showing gratitude for what they taught you about life and living.

3. Say a prayer – Let the words that are locked up in your heart and soul find a voice. Create your own prayers, say what's in your heart. If you need help finding the words, get a book like **Talking to God** by Naomi Levy which gives examples of personal prayers for a variety of situations covering the full gamut of the life cycle.

4. Write a letter – Get closure by writing a letter to the loved one you lost. Talk to him or her as if he will reply, finish any unfinished business that was left hanging, forgive or ask for forgiveness, and tell him that you love him and how you will honor his memory. Then, put the letter in your journal or burn it.

5. Share memories – Honor your loved one by sharing his or her memory at appropriate times and locations. Write down memories as they come to you. Add them to your journal and/or share them with loved ones.

6. Keep a Journal– Use your journal to express your hopes for the future, to rekindle your faith, and connection to God. Writing allows you to get in the flow with your thoughts and feelings.

7. Meet with clergy – If you have a relationship with local clergy, ask to meet with them to talk through your concerns. Ask for their advice on how to reconnect with God, how to manage your anger or despair, and how to pray with an open heart again.

Finding My Way Back to Faith Again

In addition to the above, I discovered a book by Rabbi Daniel Greyber, entitled *Faith Unravels: A Rabbi's Struggle with Grief and God*. As soon as I saw the title, I knew this book was what I had been hoping, praying, and looking for. I, too, was struggling with grief and God, and here was someone who had walked my path. I couldn't start reading quickly enough. In telling his own story of love and loss, Rabbi Greybar helped me open myself up to the power of prayer again. I wrote endlessly in my journal and took comfort in his journey back to faith, which I felt paralleled mine.

> The memory of those who kept faith in the midst of hell is a gift, a challenge to all of us. Their questions are our holy inheritance, a flashlight that shines through history into a dark room. They can help us find our way. Their enduring faith is a challenge to ours: we must never despair (Greyber).

In Judaism, we wait about a year before placing the headstone on the grave in a ceremony called an unveiling. As part of his unveiling, I delivered Richard's eulogy, which was based on passages from Rabbi Greybar's book. Rabbi Greybar helped me say goodbye to my husband while honoring the memories that Richard left in safekeeping with me. I spoke about where Richard found happiness, how we crammed 50 years of living into only 13 years, and closed with this teaching of the Rabbi's around loss and memory:

> Death is like a drop of water returning to the ocean. The water is a drop, separate from the ocean, just as we are separate from G-d while we are alive. When we die, we do not cease to be, just like the drop of water doesn't cease to be when it returns to the source. The drop of water still exists; only it isn't separate any more. Richard has returned to the oneness of the world; he is nowhere but everywhere.

Delivering the eulogy was cathartic and made me feel like I had come full circle in my grief and my spiritual life. My eulogy was a prayer thanking God for bringing me to this moment of memory and wholeness.

Review and Recommendations

Faith and hope are the manna that can sustain us when we are facing life's challenges and difficulties. Faith gives us the confidence that there are forces greater than we are in the universe protecting and supporting us. Hope gives us the belief that things will get better, no matter what. Faith and hope are the pillars of spirituality.

To rekindle your faith, think through this question: What obstacles are you facing and what is your spiritual strategy to overcome them? Where can you find hope?

In addition, you may find the following tactics useful:

- Connection points – What connects you to those you have loved and lost? Where do those intersections cross? How can you keep those connections strong?

- Be Grateful – Show gratitude for every blessing in your life and for those that others have left behind for you.

- Find the words to pray – Create prayers that reflect what's in your heart. Find the words that are locked in your heart and soul.

- Write a letter – Finish your unfinished business with a letter asking for closure. Save or destroy the letter – honoring your own needs.

- Never forget – Remember your loved one through sharing his/her memories. Tell stories, write them in your journal, and share them with loved ones.

- Start a Journal – Writing helps you get into the flow of your thoughts and feelings. It is sometimes easier to express yourself to God on paper.

- Meet with clergy – Share your concerns with clergy if you have a comfortable relationship with them. They can give you advice on how to reconnect with God, how to manage your anger or despair, and how to pray again.

Rekindling your spirit will give you back a sense of strength and comfort in your relationship with your God.

"Hope is being able to see that there is light despite all of the darkness."

-Desmond Tutu

Chapter 7
Reframing Your Failures

"Argue for your limitations they are yours."

-Richard Bach

When I was growing up, the scale of success and failure was grades. A grade of 70% or "C" was passing and success, anything below that was failure. Failure meant shame and setback. Failure was not an option in my family. Getting an "A" was the pinnacle of success, "B's" were okay, and "C's" were barely acceptable. I can only imagine what a "D" or an "F" would have meant. I'm sure in my childish view, the punishment for a "D" or an "F" would have been akin to dismemberment or death.

It's no wonder that as adults, we have no tolerance for failure and we can only see the negative side. Our experience with failure is usually limited and when we do fail at something, we take this failure personally. "Rather than saying I failed, and it feels so crappy, we move to I am a failure. We act out and shut down rather than reaching out" (Brown 47).

The end of my first marriage was my first, big failure. I chose not to look at the causes of the divorce, rather I looked at myself as a failure. I didn't accept any personal responsibility for the divorce. I blamed the failure of the marriage on my ex-husband and his poor business and financial skills, which had, lead us through bankruptcy court. This was his doing, and I was his victim. Period, end of story.

Taking on a victim mentality lets us shift blame outwards and feel sorry for ourselves and the circumstances we find ourselves in. Victimhood gives us permission to wallow in our own self-pity and to say, "woe is me" and "why me" and to ask, "What did I do to deserve this?" To find answers that satisfy that viewpoint, we look at other people, other circumstances as the source of our disappointment and our failures. We don't take any personal responsibility for what happened. We are victims awaiting rescue.

In truth, there was plenty of blame to go around for my divorce. My ex and I had grown apart. The evidence was all around if I chose to see it. We had separate interests, disparate goals, opposing parenting styles, different values. We had gone into the marriage too young and too quickly. Over the ten years of our marriage, I attended many events solo. In hindsight, I can see all of this and I understand why the marriage failed, but at the time, I wanted to lash out and to punish my ex for his inadequacies. Letting go of the anger, stress, and frustration that I felt was hard. In some twisted way, I enjoyed telling and retelling my side of the story and getting attention for going through with the divorce, gaining sole custody of our children, and doing whatever I had to in order to maintain my work and volunteer commitments.

I learned to embrace the challenges of single parenthood. I became a master at budgeting and time management ensuring that my children did not suffer along the way. I made choices like having the house cleaned so that I could spend more time playing with the children. I had friends help me create birthday parties to remember at home. I shopped sales and stretched dollars as far as I could. My ex limited his income and the amount of child support I got was meager. He held a major grudge against me and anything he could do to make my life miserable made him happy. He didn't consider the impact of his actions on the children, only on me.

Not Good Enough

I started out believing that I would never be good enough. Whenever I brought a test home from school, my father always said, "Marsha, a 98% isn't good enough." Dad thought he was being funny, but as a seven-year-old, the message I heard was, "You're not good enough." How do you go through life feeling that you are never good enough, feeling that you can never measure up to someone else's standards, unless you are perfect?

With the message "not good enough" repeating in my head like a broken record, I dove head first to victimhood. In this real-life failure, I couldn't be the one who was "not good enough," so the obvious conclusion was that someone else was "not good enough." When it came to the divorce, that someone else was my ex.

Through the years, my life has been filled with failures of all kinds. Starting with the bankruptcy and divorce and continuing with the deaths of my best friend and my husband, and loss of my job, I've faced changes, challenges, and failures that have taken away my sense of safety and security. I've had to pick myself up, brush myself off and keep moving forward. If I had let myself get caught up in the emotion of each of these losses, I would have been paralyzed by fears.

Why Do We Resist Failure?

Most people resist failure because, like me, they have been brought up to believe that getting an "A" was success and anything else was a failure. We learned that those who get the best grades, who achieve the highest scores, who make the most baskets or touchdowns, or sell the most get the accolades and awards. The rest of us are just in the background. We don't think that there is anything special about us and we don't want to be singled out for doing mediocre (but necessary) work. We want to blend in, to be middle of the road, to live our lives in peace and obscurity.

Each of us have lives that should be celebrated. Here is what is holding us back:

- Fear. Fear of the unknown. We don't know if we can survive. We don't know if we have the determination to get through. We don't know what will come next. We don't know what the outcome will be. We don't know and we don't want to find out.

- Comfort. There is comfort in staying where we are, doing what we've always done. We don't have to think about it, we just do it. We get up and do the same thing day in and day out.

- Easy. We like taking the easy way out. Like taking comfort in the status quo, it's easier to stay where we are, even if moving forward offers gifts of growth and advancement.

- Failure is scary. When we feel that slightly queasy feeling in the pit of our stomachs, it stops us in our tracks. We hold us back and find excuses to keep doing what we are doing. We don't want to ask for help, and we aren't sure who could or would help us.

- Roller coaster of emotions! An unending avalanche of emotions often accompanies failure from fear and sadness or anxiety and depression to curiosity and delight on the road to acceptance.

How to Embrace Failure

Remember what it was like when you were learning to ride a bike? You lost your balance, fell down, picked yourself back up, and tried again. Before long, you mastered balancing and were off and racing around the neighborhood. This is no different; pick yourself up, make the necessary adjustments, and try again until you get the outcome you are looking for.

Failure isn't a one-way street. Failure isn't a one-time event. Believe it or not, failure is what we need to make progress. Every failure is a chance for a do-over. Think of failure as a learning exercise and as an opportunity for personal growth. Anyone who has conducted a science experiment knows they are celebrated for creating a series of hypotheses, conducting trials, and proving or disproving their theories. This is when we learn that failure is the avenue for learning and growth. Before that, we look at learning as a binary event, all or nothing, pass or fail.

Here are seven practices to help you embrace failure:

1. Face your fears, and let them go. Below you'll find a chart with "action" and "inaction" on one axis and "best" and "worst" on the other axis. Using the questions in the chart, what are the outcomes for facing your fears? By answering these questions, you'll be poised for action, feeling more confident and comfortable in making a decision to move forward. In addition, you will understand the risks and the rewards of taking action.

	Action	Inaction
Best	What's the best thing that can happen if I do this thing?	What's the best thing that can happen if I don't do this thing?
Worst	What's the worst thing that can happen if I do this thing?	What's the worst thing that can happen if I don't do this thing?

2. Figure out the facts. Is what you are thinking really true or is the story all in your head? How do you know it's true; what's your evidence? Once you have determined the truth, what's your reaction to the real truth, and how does your reaction change your behavior?

3. Trust your gut. Sometimes other people will try to tell you what to do. And even though they mean well and have good intentions, you must learn to trust your gut. If your gut is telling you something else, follow your instincts.

4. Celebrate failures. Create a ceremony or tradition for celebrating your failures. Recognize that failures are stepping stones on the path to reaching your full potential. Find ways to celebrate moving closer to your personal goals. Have a glass of wine, get a massage, take a hike, do something that soothes your soul and gives you more energy. Keep a list of your failures and reward yourself for the efforts you are taking.

5. Ignore the naysayers. Minimize your interaction with people who are negative nellies. Hanging around with people who see the glass as half empty will enable you to hold onto negative emotions, like anger, guilt, and sadness, and to remain stuck where you are. If you want to move forward, you must open yourself up to strong, positive thinking.

6. Have a plan. Visualize where you want to go and create an action plan to get there. Don't worry if you don't have all the steps in the right order or if you miss a step. Just putting your thoughts on paper will be the momentum you need to act and move ahead.

7. Forge ahead. Revisit your goals and make adjustments so that you can continue moving forward.

Without Failure, There Is No Growth

It took me decades to recognize that without failure there is no growth. So, before we end this chapter, I'd like to share with you what I've learned from failure.

Failure has given me a stronger sense of self-confidence. I know that I can face any obstacle and figure out how to overcome or manage. I imagine my face on a punching bag clown that rebounds every time it's struck. Then, I use the energy I gain with every blow to jump back up quicker each time.

Failure has shown me that I have friends and family that I can count on in times of need. When I ask for help, I know that I'll get the support I ask for. When I need a shoulder to cry on, I know who I can call. "I found out that I had friends whose value was truly above the price of rubies" (Rowlings).

Failure has helped me grow as a person, a leader, a friend, and a mentor. I have more empathy for others as I can say, "Been there done that." I can relate my experiences to what others are facing and provide guidance from a place of personal knowledge. I can and have created programs to help others grow when I recognize what would have helped me. Hence this book.

Failure has taught me how to deal with strong emotions. I've ridden the roller coaster of emotions from the highest heights of euphoria to the lowest lows of anger and depression, and I've learned how to smooth out the bumps. I recognize when I'm stuffing my emotions back down and how to release them without harming myself or others.

Failure has demonstrated that I am a survivor. Despite all of the drama that I have faced in my life, I will not only survive but I will thrive. "Not only do we learn more from failure than from success, we learn more from bigger failures, because we scrutinize them more closely (Sandberg & Grant 43).

Review and Recommendations:

"Failure" is a scary word. When we hear "failure," we think of the shame and disappointment that come with it. We don't think about the learning and personal growth that happen.

Face your fears by asking yourself what the best and worst outcome would be. This exercise will reveal the risks of action and inaction.

Figure out the truth. We don't often challenge our thoughts. We blindly accept the conclusions we've reached. Look for evidence, and revisit your behaviors based on what's really true. This exercise is a time-out on making a bad decision.

Trust your instincts. Don't do what someone else tells you when your gut says that action is wrong. Follow your own convictions.

Celebrate your failures. While you may not want to throw a big party, find a way to honor your accomplishments or lack thereof. Recognizing your failures in a positive way helps you continue to move forward towards achieving your goals.

Ignore the naysayers. Find supporters who can help you change your own attitude. Be the one whose glass is half full instead of half empty.

Have a plan. Create a plan to get to where you want to go. When you hit an obstacle on your path, ask for help or change your course.

Push ahead. Use your failures as momentum to review and revise your action plans and goals. Making adjustments along the way is a normal part of the growth process.

Failure is a part of life. When we recognize that failure leads to growth, we can embrace failure as part of the process and survive and thrive in the face of drama.

"Try again. Fail again. Fail better."

-Samuel Beckett

Your Next Steps...

"What seems to us as bitter trials are
often blessings in disguise."

-Oscar Wilde

This book was written to inspire you to overcome life's detours and roadblocks. In this book, you have learned how to:

- restore your strength and self-image

- release your emotions and achieve acceptance

- rebuild your connections as you ask for and receive the help you need

- reclaim your place and share your gifts with the world

- recapture your optimism and with your new attitude embrace the joy and happiness all around you

- rekindle your spirit and reclaim the power of hope

- reframe your failures and recognize the opportunity for growth

In each chapter, you encountered a myriad of options to help you find your center, get back on track, and rebuild your life. My journey to wholeness took place in fits and starts across a 30-year timespan. As each new detour appeared, I discovered new paths to follow.

My advice is to choose the options that speak to your heart. Don't try to do everything at once, and above all, enjoy the journey. If you do, you will open yourself up to new experiences, new relationships, and new joy.

I truly hope that your life doesn't include as many challenges as mine. With this book in your hand, be assured that you can come back stronger no matter how crooked and broken the path you tread.

I'd love to hear how this book has helped you to live a life of resilience, thriving not merely surviving.

Send your stories of happily-ever-after endings to marsha@comebackqueen.life.

~Marsha E. Friedman

P.S. If you enjoyed this book but you still would like some additional help, I recommend visiting ComebackQueen.life. There you will discover additional tools and resources to help you as well as have the opportunity to register for a free, 30-minute consultation, where I'll help you clarify your first steps on your journey to wholeness.

Bonus Section
10 Tips to Finding
Love Again

1. Heal Yourself

You can't be emotionally available to anyone else until you have a healthy relationship with yourself, so give yourself adequate time to heal before reentering the dating scene. In her book, **Crazy Time: Surviving Divorce and Building a New Life**, Abigail Trafford refers to the healing process as Crazy Time:

> A time when your emotions take on a life of their own and you swing back and forth between wild euphoria and violent anger, ambivalence and deep depression, extreme timidity and rash actions. You can't believe how bad your life is, how terrible you feel, how overwhelming daily tasks become, how frightened you are: about money, your health, your sanity. Crazy Time is usually the very painful transition period you have to go through before you can establish a new life for yourself (Trafford).

After my divorce, I waited close to two years before I was ready to dip my toe back into the dating waters. And after losing my second husband, I waited three years. That time was critical to finding my center and healing my heart. Taking time to heal your heart too is imperative. Your contentment and self-love will show through in your profile, your voice, and your presence.

2. Develop Realistic Expectations

There are no fairy-tale princesses or knights in white, shining armor waiting to rescue you. You need to have a realistic set of expectations to begin dating. Create a list of what you want in a partner, friend, lover, or spouse, and just as importantly, what you don't want. Be sure your personal values are incorporated. Keep that list handy as you start perusing online profiles and meeting potential partners. Your list is your scorecard for a successful next relationship.

3. Tell Friends You Are Looking

My current fiancé and I have a large number of mutual friends, and although they thought we are a great match, none of them thought to introduce us because no one knew that my fiancé was interested in dating. Your friends and family have your best interest in mind, so if you're getting back into the dating world, make sure you let them know. I also suggest sharing your list from Tip Two with your friends and family members. That way they know what type of person you're looking to meet. You never know what will happen.

4. On-Line Dating

Today there are thousands of online dating sites. According to a Forbes article from 2013, there were 2500 in the U.S. alone (Zwillig). Downsides of on-line dating sites: you can't believe everything you read in a profile, pictures don't tell the whole story, and the pickings can be slim – especially as you age. Upsides of on-line dating sites: you can and will meet people whose paths you otherwise wouldn't cross.

I met both my second husband and my current fiancé via online dating apps. In 1999, the early days in internet dating, I signed up for a two-week free trial on Yenta.com (the Jewish counterpart of Matchmaker.com). After spending two evenings via dial-up (oy vey!) completing 50 multiple choice and 20 essay questions, I performed a search (within 25 miles of my zip code) that returned one profile, that of my late husband who was from Cleveland. We emailed through the site for two weeks while we checked each other's backgrounds, met for dinner, and started dating. We were married seven months later. At the time of his death, we had been married for thirteen years.

I met my current fiancé on Match.com. I liked his picture, and even though his profile was of a sports fanatic and outdoorsman, I took a chance and contacted him. In his response to my message, he shared that he was active in his synagogue, enabling me to vet him through a mutual friend. Our paths would not have crossed if we hadn't met through Match.com. We dated for a year before our engagement and plan to marry in the spring of 2019, in the presence of our children, grandchildren, and closest friends.

5. Stay Safe

Safety is a primary issue when you are meeting someone you don't know for the first time. First, I suggest meeting at a neutral, public location such as Panera or Starbucks. Second, let someone else know where you'll be, who you'll be meeting (name, phone number, email address, etc.), and what time you'll be home. Also, have a safe word or phrase, just in case something uncomfortable happens and you need to call for help. Third, even if you and your match are both avid wine, craft beer, or martini drinkers, don't be tempted. Alcohol dulls the senses and can knock you off your game. Don't let alcohol have any influence on your decision making. Lastly, have an exit strategy. Even if you seem to have hit it off via email, text, and phone, meeting in person isn't the same thing. If there's no chemistry, bail out.

6. Get to Know One Another

If you feel chemistry between you, how do you get to know one another? Try the app, "36 Questions." The app has a series of questions for you and your new friend to take turns answering. The questions become more intimate as you progress and require openness, honesty, and vulnerability. By the time you finish, you'll know a bit about each other and have a better idea if you want to move forward with this new relationship.

The app is based on Mandy Catron's *New York Times* article entitled, "To Fall in Love with Anyone, Do This" (Catron, 2015). In that article, Mandy shares the research behind the questions and her own experience asking them to a friend.

7. Give Each Other Space

As mature adults, you and your partner are coming into this relationship with a lot of history. While you are creating a new identity as a couple, cherish your similarities and honor the differences that each of you bring. Sharing your common interests and learning from each other is part of growing the relationship. But it is equally important to give each other space and time to pursue your individual interests. This time apart will strengthen the relationship.

8. Introducing the Family

If you are a single parent with children at home, deciding when to introduce your romantic partner can be tricky. You don't want to make an introduction too early, as you are still getting to know one another, and you don't want your children to become emotionally attached to someone who may not be in the picture for the long term. At the same time, you want your children to accept the fact that you are dating and that there might be a new adult in their lives. If you have adult children, this introduction can be somewhat less problematic as you probably don't share the same residence as your children. Take your time and discuss with your partner to decide when you want to introduce family into the relationship.

9. Be Open and Honest

Be open and honest, and know your limits. You must be willing to tell your partner what you need in the relationship, how you want to be treated, and where you have limitations. In addition to chemistry and romance, developing a long, lasting relationship requires open communication, self-awareness, and a sense of humor.

10. Not Ready to Date Yet?

Maybe you're on the cusp but not ready to date yet. If this is the case, then I suggest downloading the "Meetup" app and finding a group that piques your interest. Meetup groups cover a wide range of activities from health/wellness and sport/fitness to food/drink and games. The benefit of a Meetup is that the activities are designed for a group, and you won't be doing them on your own. This is a great place to meet people and make friends without going on a date.

About the Author

Marsha Friedman, MLS, RCC™, DTM, is a leadership and personal development coach, professional speaker, and trainer with more than 30 years in corporate America. She brings a broad range of business experience from finance to customer service and operations to organizational development.

Marsha is a lifelong learner with a BS in Accounting from Miami University and a Masters Liberal Studies in Organizational Leadership from Fort Hays State University. She holds certifications as a Registered Corporate Coach™, Master Trainer, Myers Briggs and DiSC facilitator, and Distinguished Toastmaster. Marsha is a facilitator at The Corporate University, Kent State and co-facilitator of Summit Networking Group for executive level job seekers.

Marsha is an active member of Athena International, the International Coaches Federation, and Toastmasters International. She serves as Treasurer of Beth El Congregation and co-chairs Knitzvah (knitting & crocheting for local charities).

Marsha is a mother/step-mother of four and grandmother of nine who enjoys cooking and sharing meals with her family and friends as well as working out. She is an avid reader, theater-goer, and film buff and is passionate about dark chocolate and good wine!

Looking for a speaker who can connect with everyone in your audience?

Then look no further!

Marsha engages her audiences with her natural humor and charm and "is a clear and articulate speaker who is able to connect with a wide variety of audiences."

Marsha's five, most popular topics include:

- **Benefits of Failure:** Learn The 5 Keys to Unlock the Benefits of Failure and Turn Your Greatest Failures into Your Greatest Successes

- **Not Good Enough:** Exploring the Underpinnings of Self-Confidence, So You Can Light A Fire That Will Take You to the Top!

- **Your Full Potential:** The 6 Practices You Need to Stop and the 6 Practices You Need to Start to Reach Your Full Potential.

- **Resilience - The Magic Ingredient:** How to Tap into Your Reserves of Resilience to Overcome the Roadblocks That Life Throws in Your Way.

- **Connecting the Dots**: How Creating a Personal Value Proposition Will Increase Your Engagement and Productivity

Marsha is available for both live and online events. She will give your audience members valuable insight and actionable takeaways that they can use immediately.

Book Marsha Friedman today by contacting her at: 330-603-1890 or marsha@comebackqueen.life or visit ComebackQueen.life.

See What Other Event Planners Have Said About Working with Marsha...

"Marsha's ability to deliver training in an effective and engaging way was remarkable. She quickly mastered our training content and was able to hit the ground running. Marsha's unique gift of relating to a diverse group of people helped us deliver our program to hundreds of employees. Her professionalism and enthusiasm greatly contributed the success of our training effort. Marsha is an invaluable resource whom we hope to partner with again the future!"

Carrie Ball, Manager of Talent Management, US Acute Care Solutions

"Marsha's service and personalization of our education has been astronomical to our success. Marsha is creative in her thinking, reliable, and consistently exceeded our expectations! We are keeping Marsha on speed dial for future projects!"

Christine Boulden, Director of Quality and Risk Management, Summa Rehab Hospital

"Marsha is a clear and articulate presenter who is able to connect with a wide variety of audiences. She projects unparalleled energy and confidence, making her messages distinct and relatable."

Jerry Gilin, Director of Training, DRB Systems

"Marsha is an engaging speaker who brings a wealth of knowledge and experience that helps students accelerate 'real world' application of management and leadership processes."

Chad Cook Adjunct Profession Baldwin Wallace University

Book Marsha Friedman today by contacting her at:
330-603-1890 or marsha@comebackqueen.life
or visit ComebackQueen.life

Comeback Queen Playlist

Title	Artist
Brave	Sara Bareilles
Rise	Katy Perry
I Hope You Dance	Lee Ann Womack
Stronger (What Doesn't Kill You)	Kelly Clarkson
Roar	Katy Perry
Hero	Mariah Carey
Wind Beneath My Wings	Bette Midler
When You Believe	Whitney Houston, Mariah Carey
Don't Stop Believin'	Journey
Have it All	Jason Mraz
I'm Still Standing	Taron Egerton
Defying Gravity	Kristen Chenoweth, Idina Menzel
Keep Holding On	Avril Lavigne
Hands on the Wheel	Beth Sass
Go the Distance	Michael Bolton
I Can See Clearly Now	Johnny Nash
Let It Go	Idina Menzel
Hit Me With Your Best Shot	Pat Benatar
This One's for the Girls	Martina McBride

Title	Artist
You Will Be Found	Dear Evan Hanson, Broadway Cast Album
Never Give Up	Sia
I Won't Back Down	Tom Petty
Lean on Me	Bill Withers
Just the Way You Are	Bruno Mars
Breathe	Anna Nalick
Fighter	Christina Aguilera
This is Me	Keala Settle
Keep Your Head Up	Andy Grammer
Warrior	Demi Lovato
I Will Survive	Gloria Gaynor
You Will Be Found	Dear Evan Hansen, Broadway Cast Album
Glitter in the Air	Pink
Girl on Fire	Alicia Keys
Fight Song	Rachel Platten
Skyscraper	Demi Lovato
You Gotta Be	Des'ree

Works Cited

Barrie, J. Peter Pan. New York: Coterie Classics, 2016.

Brown, B. Rising Strong: The reckoning. The rumble. The revolution. New York: Random House, 2015.

Catron, M. "To Fall in Love with Anyone Do This." New York Times 9 June 2015.

Greyber, D. Faith Unravels: A rabbi's struggle with grief and god. Eugene, OR: Wipf & Stock Publishers, 2012.

Kubler-Ross, E. On Death and Dying: what the dying have to teach doctors, nurses, clergy & their own families. New York: Scribner, 1969.

Kushner, H. S. Conquering fear: Living boldly in an uncertain world. New York: Alfred A. Knopf, 2009.

McGonigal, K. "How to Make Stress your Friend." TED Global 2013. June 2013. <http://www.ted.com/talks/kelly_mcgonigal_how_to_make_stress_your_friend>

Mrosko, T. "Nine elements of resiliency." Cleveland Plain Dealer 31 December 2014.

Rowlings, J. K. "The Fringe Benefits of Failure, and the Importance of Imagination." The Harvard Gazette. 5 June 2008. <https://news.harvard.edu/gazette/story/2008/06/text-of-j-k-rowling-speech/>.

Sandberg, S., & Grant, A. Option B: Facing adversity, building resilience, and finding joy. New York: Alfred A Knopf, 2017.

Seery, M. D. "Resilience: A silver lining to experiencing adverse life events?" Current Directions in Psychological Science 2011: 20(6), 390-394.

Shpancer, N. "What doesn't kill you makes you weaker: A history of hardship is not a life asset." Insight Therapy 21 August 2010.

"So Nietzsche was right: what doesn't kill you makes you stronger, scientists find." Daily Mail Reporter. 18 December 2011. <http://www.dailymail.co.uk/sciencetech/article-2075908/So-Nietzsche-WAS-right-What-doesnt-kill-makes-stronger-scientists-find.html>.

Trafford, A. Crazy Time: surviving divorce and building a new life. New York: Wm Morris Paperbacks, 2014.

Zwillig, M. "How Many More On-Line Dating Sites Do We Need?" Forbes. 1 March 2013. <https://www.forbes.com/sites/martinzwilling/2013/03/01/how-many-more-online-dating-sites-do-we-need/#762200878824>.

Made in the USA
Coppell, TX
15 March 2021

51774081R00059